The Treasure Hunt

Greenfield School PTA FAIR

Help Raise Money For Your School!

Karen King
Illustrated by Reggie Holladay

Rigby®

A Harcourt Achieve Imprint

www.Rigby.com
1-800-531-5015

"Ready, you two?" asked Mom.

"Yes!" shouted Karen joyfully.

"I left my hat in my bedroom, so I'll just go and get it," said Mark.

"Hurry up or we'll be late for the fair!"
Karen called to Mark as he rolled his
wheelchair quickly along the hall and into
his bedroom.

Mark returned a few minutes later wearing
his favorite gray baseball hat. "I'm all set,"
he said.

The PTA had planned the school fair, and Karen and Mark's mom was in charge of the baked goods stand. She gave Karen and Mark some money to spend and said, "Have fun, but stay on the school grounds and stay together."

"OK," they promised.

The two children looked around at all there was to see and do. Some of the stands had things for sale, and some had games to play with prizes to win. Karen and Mark both wanted to win a prize.

"Bet I win one first," said Karen.

"No chance!" Mark replied.

As they neared the basketball game, Karen suggested, "Let's give it a try!"

She went first and almost got the ball into the hoop but just missed. Then it was Mark's turn. He put the ball in his lap as he moved his wheelchair in position to shoot the ball into the basket.

Mark missed too, so Mr. Timms asked if they wanted to try again.

"No, thanks," said Karen. "We'll see what else we can try."

Mark saw some children throwing beanbags at bottles and thought it looked like fun.

"Catch," said Mr. Smith with a smile as he threw Mark three beanbags. "If you knock the bottles down, you win a prize," he explained.

Karen watched as Mark threw each of the beanbags. The first throw was a miss, the second throw was a miss, and the third throw was a miss!

"Watch the pro," said Karen as she prepared to take her turn. She didn't hit the bottles, either.

"Good try for both of you," said Mr. Smith. "You can each have a bookmark for being such good sports."

As Mark and Karen thanked him and took the bookmarks, they spotted the ring toss booth nearby.

"All we have to do is throw a ring over the prize we want to win—that sounds easy enough," said Karen.

But it looked easier than it was.

"We'll never win a prize," said Karen.

"Let's see if Mom will give us a snack," said Mark, wheeling himself in the direction of the baked goods booth.

Mom was happy to see them. "Are you enjoying yourselves?" she asked as she put out a batch of homemade granola bars.

"Yes, but we haven't won a prize yet," Karen said while chewing a mouthful of granola bar.

"Why don't you enter the Treasure Hunt?" suggested Mom as she waved at Mrs. Castillo.

"What do we have to do?" asked Mark.

"You're given clues, and you work together
to find the answers, collecting things as you
go along," explained Mom. "The first pair
back with all their treasures wins a prize."

Mark and Karen hurried over to Mrs.
Castillo's table where many other children
were waiting.

"You're just in time," said Mrs. Castillo. "Here are all of the clues for the three things you need to find. All of the items are at the different booths."

Mrs. Castillo gave everyone a yellow sticker, explaining, "Wear this so that everyone knows you're in the Treasure Hunt. That way you can ask for the things you need."

Then she gave every team a bag, and Mark and Karen set off, holding onto their clues and bag.

They looked at the first clue.

Finding your way is easy
if you have this with you.
See Mr. Brown's table
for the answer to this clue.

They looked around for Mr. Brown and saw him at the book booth. They hurried over.

"What do you think it is?" asked Karen, looking at the pile of books.

Can you solve the clue?
Turn the page to see if you are right.

"It's the atlas!" said Mark. "Atlases have maps, which show you how to get to places. So atlases help you find your way."

Mr. Brown smiled and gave them the atlas. "Well done," he said as Karen put the book in the bag.

She and Mark looked at the next clue.

It has hands that can't feel
and makes a loud sound.
Try Mrs. Yeoh's booth for something
blue and round.

"What can that be?" asked Mark as they looked around.

Can you solve the clue?
Turn the page to see if you are right.

"I know—the alarm clock!" shouted Karen. "It's blue, round, makes a loud sound, and has hands that can't feel."

Mrs. Yeoh smiled and handed them the alarm clock. "Good luck with the other clues," she said.

Karen and Mark then read the last clue.

It's long and thin, dark and light.

This keeps you warm day or night.

Look on Mr. Cortez' table.

Find it if you're able.

They both stared at all the things on Mr. Cortez' table and wondered what it could be.

Can you solve the clue?
Turn the page to see if you are right.

"The black and white scarf!" they both shouted at once.

"Good job!" said Mr. Cortez.

Karen stuffed the scarf into their bag. "Come on, let's get going!" she said to Mark, and they hurried back to the Treasure Hunt table.

"We've found everything!" they shouted.

"Let me check," said Mrs. Castillo as she emptied the bag and looked at each item. "Hooray!" she cheered. "You won!"

"And here's another game you can play," she said, handing them their prize.

Karen and Mark grinned. "Way to go!" Mark said as he gave his sister a high five.

"We make a great team when we work together," added Karen.